Before you start revising for an exam, you need to find out _____

Find out what you're gonna be tested on

Below are the places to go to get a decent course outline for all your subjects.

Your teacher is your best resource. He or she should be able to give you course specifications, or a course outline they've worked out.

1) The clear and concise CGP Revision guides are a great starting place.

www.cgpbooks.co.uk

Blatant CGP advert — see inside back cover.

2) For GCSEs or 'A' levels you need the course specification (syllabus).

OCR: www.ocr.org.uk,
AQA: www.aqa.org.uk,
Edexcel: www.edexcel.org.uk,
Welsh: www.wjec.co.uk,
Irish: www.ccea.org.uk
— select the qualification and the subject.

Did you just let one go?

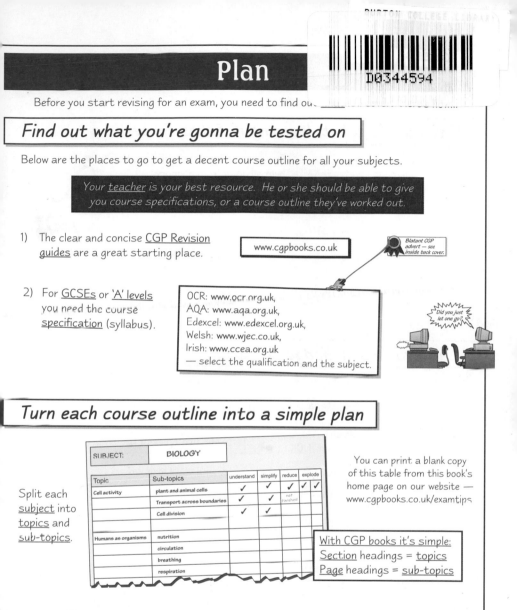

Turn each course outline into a simple plan

Split each subject into topics and sub-topics.

SUBJECT:	BIOLOGY	understand	simplify	reduce	explode
Topic	Sub-topics				
Cell activity	plant and animal cells	✓	✓	✓	✓ ✓
	Transport across boundaries	✓	✓	not finished	
	Cell division	✓	✓		
Humans as organisms	nutrition				
	circulation				
	breathing				
	respiration				

You can print a blank copy of this table from this book's home page on our website — www.cgpbooks.co.uk/examtips

With CGP books it's simple:
Section headings = topics
Page headings = sub-topics

Make a revision time-table

Without a time-table you'll revise some stuff a lot, miss out other bits and have a mad rush at the end. Follow these rules and use the examples on this book's home page on our website.

1) Stick in all the non revision stuff first — school, sleep, frisbee practice, exams.

2) Split up the remaining bits of each day or evening into 1 to 1½ hour revision chunks. Do a different subject per chunk. Aim for 2 chunks each evening.

3) Set yourself targets for each week and stick to them.

Understand

It's mad trying to learn something <u>before</u> you understand it. First understand, then learn.

If you don't get it, learning it takes forever...

1) This example will prove it to you. Read the words in the following box, cover the page and try to write them <u>all</u> down from <u>memory</u>.

> my earache — my ears are bleeding because my mother keeps singing.

2) Now do the same thing with this one:

> ym caheaer — are singing. bleeding my because ears my keeps mother

3) Unless you're a robot, you got more of the <u>**first one**</u> right — because it made sense to you, you <u>**understood**</u> it. It's possible to learn the second one, but it'd take <u>ages</u>.

...and you'll still bodge the exams

1) You can learn the sentence below word for word <u>without</u> understanding it.

> Some bacteria are parasitic, some are saprophytic.

2) If you get this question in the exam you could probably answer it <u>OK</u>.

> 1. Name two types of bacteria. (2 marks)

3) But if you get asked this you <u>won't</u> have a clue and you'll lose 2 marks.

> 1. How do saprophytic bacteria help get rid of waste? (2 marks)

4) If you'd spent <u>2 minutes</u> finding out what saprophytic means, you'd have 2 marks. Just use all that nose-picking time to <u>understand</u> stuff and you'll get a better grade.

So before you start revising a topic...

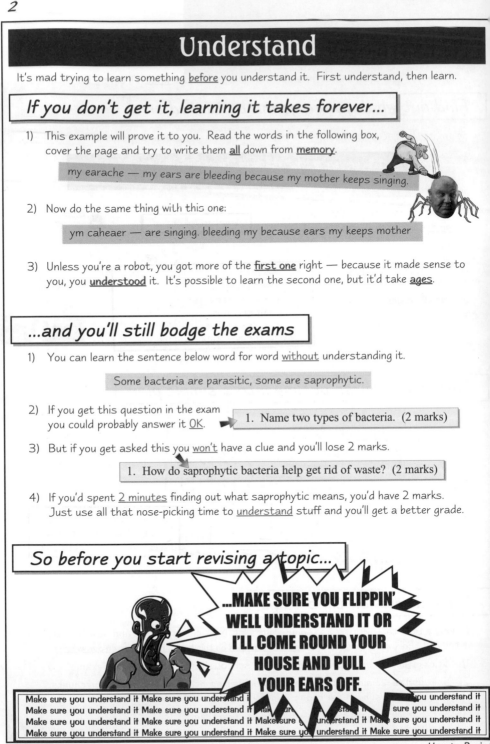

...MAKE SURE YOU FLIPPIN' WELL UNDERSTAND IT OR I'LL COME ROUND YOUR HOUSE AND PULL YOUR EARS OFF.

Make sure you understand it Make sure you understand it ... you understand it
Make sure you understand it Make sure you understand it ... sure you understand it
Make sure you understand it Make sure you understand it Make sure you understand it Make sure you understand it
Make sure you understand it Make sure you understand it Make sure you understand it Make sure you understand it

Understanding

Revise

Once you understand a topic you need to <u>remember it</u>. People get it into their heads that revision is just reading stuff over and over. BORING. Forget that. Do it this way.

Take one sub-topic at a time from your plan and follow this simple, 4-step brain improvement plan for a fuller, more active exam life.

Bernie, the other buttock's at it now

① SIMPLIFY SEE PAGES 4 – 7

How
Take your sub-topic, put it into fewer words and draw simplified diagrams. I've given you two examples of what I mean on the next four pages.

Why
It makes you read through the sub-topic in detail so you can decide how to simplify it. You get more of the subject into your head than if you just read it through.

② REDUCE SEE PAGES 8 – 11

How
Reduce the simplified sub-topic into a smaller wad of info. When you've simplified and reduced all the sub-topics in a topic, go on to number 3.

Why
Going over what you've done reinforces the memories in your head. By actively thinking about how to reduce it, you'll make strong memories quickly.

③ EXPLODE THE TOPIC SEE PAGES 12 – 13

How
Show all the small wads of info for one topic on one page. When you've done this for all the topics in a subject, go on to number 4.

Why
Drawing this out makes you go over every sub-topic again. It also gives you an overview of the whole topic to jog and test that bag of neurones in your skull.

④ EXPLODE THE SUBJECT SEE PAGES 14 – 15

How
Like the topic explosion, but this time showing the whole subject in a monster picture on one page.

Why
Gives you everything you need to cover one subject on one bit of paper. It won't seem as scary or stressful when you can see what you're dealing with.

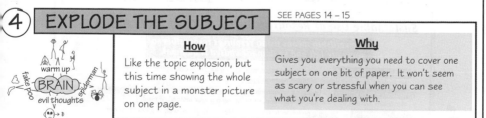

READ THIS — THIS IS VERY IMPORTANT — READ THIS — THIS IS VERY IMPORTANT

As soon as you START this you ARE revising. This is NOT preparation BEFORE revision, THIS IS REVISION, so concentrate and DON'T rush through it without thinking. (I'll stop shouting now)

Simplify

Start with the right stuff

1) A CGP revision guide gives you a fantastic <u>starting point</u>
   — whole sub-topics like the one below are often on a single page.

Blatant CGP
advert — see
inside back cover.

2) If you need to, you can <u>add in notes</u> from your class book <u>before</u> simplifying it.

3) The page below is a sub-topic from our <u>GCSE geography</u> book. On the next page I've shown you how it can be simplified.

The Use and Abuse of Resources

The growing population and increasing standard of living is putting greater demands on the world's resources. A <u>bigger global</u> population needs more resources — at the very least people need <u>food</u> and <u>water supplies</u>. Increasing <u>standards of living</u> uses more goods and services causing resources to be <u>used up faster</u>.

Quarrying means Digging for Land Resources

1) Quarries <u>spoil</u> the landscape, and the <u>land</u> can't always be reclaimed.
2) <u>Rock</u>, <u>sand</u> and <u>gravel</u> are important resources, but to get at them a lot of <u>unusable</u> material has to be removed first.
3) <u>Metal ores</u> make up only a <u>tiny fraction</u> of the rocks in which they are found — the rest is <u>waste</u>. Other waste is <u>dumped</u> in quarries.
4) Some <u>disused quarries</u> have become very important habitats for <u>wildlife</u> — they are also useful places for learning about <u>geology</u>.

Is that ALL?

Conservation and Recycling Provide for the Future

1) <u>Reducing demand</u> for fossil fuels means they'll <u>last longer</u>, and <u>reduce</u> the harmful <u>effects</u> of using them — eg. smaller cars with more efficient engines use less fuel; insulating the lofts of houses reduces the use of heating fuel.
2) <u>Conserving the soil</u> by preventing erosion will provide food for future generations.
3) <u>Recycling</u> metals and paper means using <u>less raw material</u> and <u>cuts energy use</u> too — eg. metals and glass can be <u>reclaimed</u> from scrap cars; papers can be <u>re-processed</u> into paper bags and toilet paper.

Managing Resources is a Balancing Act

1) Some resources <u>aren't</u> always <u>available</u> where they're most wanted — the fastest-growing demand for water in the UK is in the south-east, the highest rainfall is in the north and west.
2) There <u>won't</u> always be <u>enough</u> to go round — although <u>LEDCs</u> produce <u>much</u> of the world's resources, <u>most</u> are used by <u>MEDCs</u>. LEDC development means they want <u>more</u> resources.
3) Multinational companies <u>fear</u> that reduction in consumption will <u>reduce profits</u> — eg. BP, which is involved in the search for new oil supplies off the Falkland Islands.
4) <u>Research</u> into alternative materials and energy resources is <u>time-consuming</u> and <u>expensive</u>.

Sustainable Use of Resources Relies on Good Stewardship

Stewardship means using resources responsibly so some are left and so damage caused is minimal.

1) Resource conservation — Using resources carefully to <u>slow</u> our consumption of them, eg. making cars and power stations more <u>efficient</u> so you use less fuel.
2) Resource substitution — Changing resources for more <u>sustainable</u> ones, eg. using recyclable aluminium instead of steel for making cans, or using wind power instead of coal.
3) Pollution control — <u>Limiting</u> pollution to reduce problems like global warming and acid rain.
4) Recycling — Used to reduce the amount of <u>waste</u> produced and as part of <u>resource conservation</u>.

The resource problem is tiring — so conserve your energy...

The tricky thing about this page is making sure you can fit it all together. All you really need to know is <u>what</u> they are, how they're <u>abused</u> and the difficulties of <u>managing</u> them. Five mini-essays then, please.

Simplify

Get it all on to one page or less

Sub-topics from non-CGP books or from your class notes will be more wordy than this one. They'll need more work, but you should be able to get each one on a single page.

The use and abuse of resources

Growing pop. + increased standard of living - greater demands on worlds resources.

Quarrying (digging for land resources)
1) Spoil landscape sometimes for good.
2) Rock, sand, gravel - unusable material removed first.
3) Metal ore - loads of waste rock, dumped
4) Disused quarries - geology education, important wildlife habitats

Conservation / recycling
1) Reducing demand - last longer, reduce harmful effects eg efficiency / less heating
2) Conserving soil - preventing erosion - future food
3) Recycling (metals, paper) - use less raw material - use less energy to reprocess

Managing Resources
1) Resources aren't always where they're needed eg water demand London but most water in north west of the UK.
2) Not always enough to go round. LEDCs produce most, MEDCs use most. LEDCs will need more as they develop.
3) Multinationals fear reduction in consumption will reduce profits. eg BP Oil in Falklands.
4) Research into alternative materials / energy resources - time consuming, expensive

Sustainable use of resources - good stewardship
1) Resource Conservation - careful use eg efficient cars, power stations
2) Resource Substitution - change to more sustainable resources eg
3) Pollution control - limiting to reduce global warming, acid rain
4) Recycling - reduce waste and use less resource

Sustainable = kept at a steady level without running out

DON'T JUST COPY IT OUT. Copying it out bypasses your brain. If it doesn't even go into your brain it's got CENSORED all chance of staying there. If you want to copy, use a photocopier; if you want to revise, use your brain.

1) Read through each section, pick out the important bits and reduce down the words.
2) Use numbered points — they're great for organising info into chunks.
3) Have a go at using pictures to show bits of info. They don't have to be good, just as long as you know what they are. Coming up with them helps you remember stuff.
4) If you don't understand any words, look them up and write out what they mean in your own words, at the bottom of the page.

When you've simplified a topic — test yourself

1) Cover everything up.
2) Get a blank sheet of paper and write out as much of the sub-topic as you can.
3) Use your simplified notes to add things you missed and correct things you got wrong
4) You won't remember everything yet, probably just the headings and a few details.

Simplify

The last example showed you how to simplify sub-topics that are <u>mostly words</u>. These two pages show you how to tackle sub-topics based on <u>diagrams</u>. The page below shows a skinless man showing off his <u>digestive system</u>.

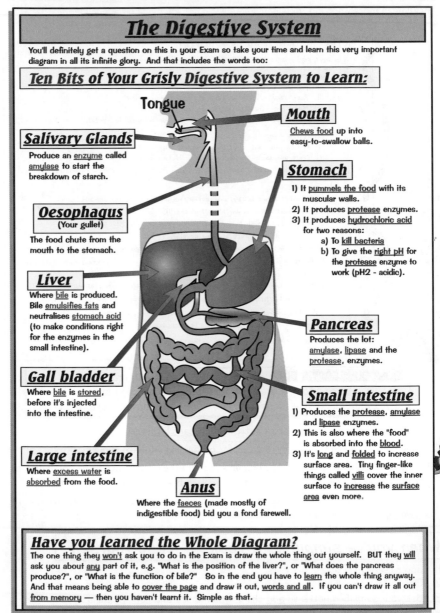

The Digestive System

You'll definitely get a question on this in your Exam so take your time and learn this very important diagram in all its infinite glory. And that includes the words too:

Ten Bits of Your Grisly Digestive System to Learn:

Tongue

Mouth
<u>Chews food</u> up into easy-to-swallow balls.

Salivary Glands
Produce an <u>enzyme</u> called <u>amylase</u> to start the breakdown of starch.

Stomach
1) It <u>pummels the food</u> with its muscular walls.
2) It produces <u>protease</u> enzymes.
3) It produces <u>hydrochloric acid</u> for two reasons:
   a) To <u>kill bacteria</u>
   b) To give the <u>right pH</u> for the <u>protease</u> enzyme to work (pH2 - acidic).

Oesophagus
(Your gullet)
The food chute from the mouth to the stomach.

Liver
Where <u>bile</u> is produced. Bile <u>emulsifies fats</u> and neutralises <u>stomach acid</u> (to make conditions right for the enzymes in the small intestine).

Pancreas
Produces the lot: <u>amylase</u>, <u>lipase</u> and the <u>protease</u>, enzymes.

Gall bladder
Where <u>bile</u> is <u>stored</u>, before it's injected into the intestine.

Small intestine
1) Produces the <u>protease</u>, <u>amylase</u> and <u>lipase</u> enzymes.
2) This is also where the "food" is absorbed into the <u>blood</u>.
3) It's <u>long</u> and <u>folded</u> to increase surface area. Tiny finger-like things called <u>villi</u> cover the inner surface to <u>increase</u> the <u>surface area</u> even more.

Large intestine
Where <u>excess water</u> is <u>absorbed</u> from the food.

Anus
Where the <u>faeces</u> (made mostly of indigestible food) bid you a fond farewell.

Have you learned the Whole Diagram?
The one thing they <u>won't</u> ask you to do in the Exam is draw the whole thing out yourself. BUT they <u>will</u> ask you about <u>any</u> part of it, e.g. "What is the position of the liver?", or "What does the pancreas produce?", or "What is the function of bile?" So in the end you have to <u>learn</u> the whole thing anyway. And that means being able to <u>cover the page</u> and draw it out, <u>words and all</u>. If you can't draw it all out <u>from memory</u> — then you haven't learnt it. Simple as that.

Simplify

If you see a whopping diagram like digestion, <u>don't panic</u>, it's actually easier to revise than a load of text. You can simplify the picture and <u>tag on</u> all the info you need.

Simplifying diagrams

Simplifying for revision is all about showing all the important bits of a topic in a simple way — it <u>**DOES NOT**</u> mean just missing out bits at random.

1) Go over the diagram and decide which are the <u>important bits</u>.
   In this case: the name, function and order of digestive organs are the important bits.

2) Draw <u>simple</u> but recognisable pictures to show what's going on.
   In this case, I've shown the organs that food travels through in the correct order and then added on the organs that provide or store digestive juices.

3) <u>Label</u> diagrams to show what the different bits do and how they fit together.

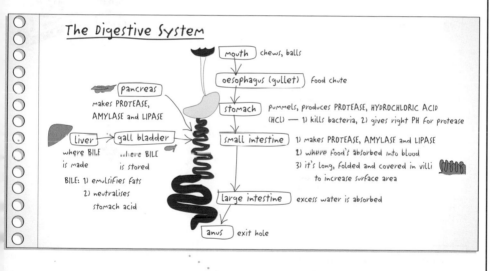

The Digestive System

- (mouth) chews, balls
- (oesophagus (gullet)) food chute
- (pancreas) makes PROTEASE, AMYLASE and LIPASE
- (stomach) pummels, produces PROTEASE, HYDROCHLORIC ACID (HCL) — 1) kills bacteria, 2) gives right PH for protease
- (liver) where BILE is made
- (gall bladder) where BILE is stored
  BILE: 1) emulsifies fats
  2) neutralises stomach acid
- (small intestine) 1) makes PROTEASE, AMYLASE and LIPASE
  2) where food's absorbed into blood
  3) it's long, folded and covered in villi to increase surface area
- (large intestine) excess water is absorbed
- (anus) exit hole

Simplifying the words

1) Decide on some <u>simple rules</u> and stick to them. I've stuck all the organs in boxes, capitalised all digestive juices and written important words in red.

2) Keep your writing <u>concise</u>, but don't miss anything out.

3) <u>Add</u> pictures (like the villi). Revision's all about keeping your brain engaged and if you have to think about what to draw, your head machine will be working hard.

8

Reduce

The next step is to take your simplified sub-topic and <u>reduce</u> it down into a memory <u>prompt</u>. Actively thinking how to reduce it will strengthen your memory and you'll be left with a small prompt you can use to remember and test the <u>whole</u> sub-topic.

Reduce the sub-topic down to key words

1) Choose a key word for <u>each point</u>.

2) It should be a word that has something to do with the point being made — <u>not</u> words like "a, it, the, when".

3) For some points it may not be obvious. Choose a word that'll help <u>you</u> remember the rest of the information (eg for point 2 of the quarry bit I chose "rock"). For most of them I've picked the <u>first word</u>, but it can be other words if they stick out more.

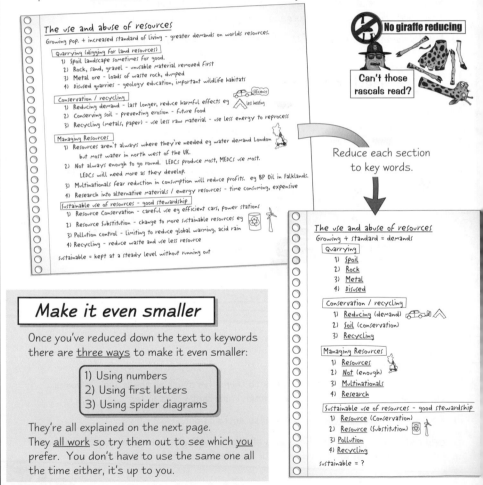

Reduce each section to key words.

Make it even smaller

Once you've reduced down the text to keywords there are <u>three ways</u> to make it even smaller:

> 1) Using numbers
> 2) Using first letters
> 3) Using spider diagrams

They're all explained on the next page.
They <u>all work</u> so try them out to see which <u>you</u> prefer. You don't have to use the same one all the time either, it's up to you.

Reduce

Option 1: Reduce the key words to numbers

1) Reduce the sub-topic to just <u>section headings</u> with the <u>number of points</u> written after each one.

2) Or instead of section headings you can use <u>pictures</u> with the numbers <u>included</u> to show each section.
   Eg for quarrying, draw something like this:

Use & abuse of resources GP + S = D
Quarrying ④
Conservation ③
Resources ④
Sustainable ④

Option 2: Use the first letter strategy

The first letter strategy involves turning each section into a <u>list of first letters</u> and then combining them in an <u>interesting sentence</u> you'll remember <u>easily</u>.

1) Reduce the <u>section heading</u> and each <u>key word</u> to the first letter of each word.

2) Use the first letter strategy to remember it — use the letters to start each word of a memorable sentence (see the examples below). <u>Funny</u> or <u>rude</u> sentences work best.

3) It's even better if you can <u>connect</u> the sentences somehow like I've done with "rats".

Tip: If the order of points isn't important you can rearrange the letters so it's easier to make a sentence, but always keep the topic name at the front - eg I've switched around the quarrying bit below.

Reduced to first letters

The use and abuse of resources GP + S = D
Quarrying S R M D
Conservation R S R
Resources R N M R
Sustainable R R P R

Memorable sentences

Use & abuse of resources ④ GP + S = D
Queen Rats Drink Monkey Sick
Clever Rats Sell Rum
Roland Rat Nuked My Raincoat
Smelly Rats Remember Peter Rabbit

Option 3: Draw it all in a spider diagram

1) Stick the name of the sub-topic in a blob in the <u>middle</u> of the page.

2) Draw each section as a <u>branch</u> off this blob.

3) Use the first letters of the keywords to show the details on <u>smaller branches</u>.

4) Use <u>pictures</u> if you prefer, but <u>don't</u> spend longer than a couple of minutes on each one.

Working out how to show something as a picture helps you learn it. Pictures also stick in some people's minds better than words, numbers or letters.

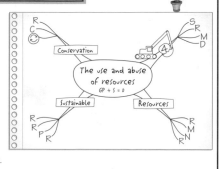

R C ☺
Conservation
S R M D
The use and abuse of resources GP + S = D
Sustainable
Resources
R R P R
R M M N R

If you're short of time when you get to this stage, skip the explosion bits, test yourself loads with the prompts

Reduce

Reduce your diagrams down to <u>quick line drawings</u> with <u>prompts</u> for each label.

Reduce the diagram to simple lines and prompts

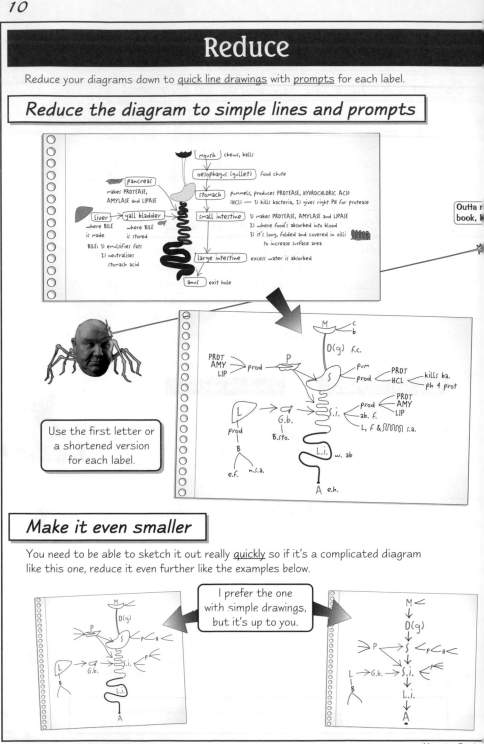

Use the first letter or a shortened version for each label.

Outta r book, b

Make it even smaller

You need to be able to sketch it out really <u>quickly</u> so if it's a complicated diagram like this one, reduce it even further like the examples below.

I prefer the one with simple drawings, but it's up to you.

Reduce

By reducing down your notes you've done <u>two</u> things: 1) Thinking about how to reduce things has stuck them more <u>firmly</u> in your memory; 2) The simple sketches or notes will act as <u>memory prompts</u> for testing and quickly reproducing in <u>exams</u>.

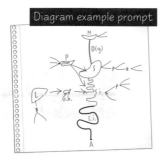

Diagram example prompt

Text example prompt

<u>Use & abuse of resources</u> ④ GP + S = D

Queen Rats Drink Monkey Sick
Clever Rats Sell Rum
Roland Rat Nuked My Raincoat
Smelly Rats Remember Peter Rabbit

Test yourself using your prompts

Follow these 5 points and you'll be able to remember an <u>entire</u> sub-topic from <u>one small prompt</u>. That's one tiny step from bringing it all back in an <u>exam</u>.

1) Use your prompt to <u>recall</u> (out loud) as much detail as you can about the sub-topic. If you can't remember bits, just move on and recall everything you can.

2) Turn back to your notes and read out <u>anything</u> you missed out or got wrong.

3) Cover up your full notes again and use your prompt to <u>write out</u> all the information.

4) <u>Check</u> against your full notes and make any corrections.

5) Keep doing 3) and 4) until you don't get <u>anything</u> wrong or miss <u>anything</u> out.

Turn a blank page into full notes

It's time to remove the prompts and start with nothing — just like in the exam.

1) Take a long hard look at your prompt and then <u>cover it up</u>.

2) Take a <u>blank</u> piece of paper and try to sketch out your prompt.

3) Check it against your real prompt and make any corrections.

4) Use this prompt to write out <u>all</u> the detail.

5) Do it <u>again</u>. Start with a blank piece of paper, sketch out the prompt and then write out all the detail. Keep doing it until you can do it quickly without mistakes.

Explode the **Topic**

When you've done all the prompts for a <u>topic</u> draw out a giant <u>spider diagram</u> to show them all.
(P.S. I used the word "explode" because I've just seen *Die Hard* on the telly.)

Draw a topic explosion

Work in <u>pencil</u> first so you can make changes if you need to.

1) Write the <u>topic name</u> in a blob in the middle of the page.
2) Draw one branch away from the blob for each <u>sub-topic</u>.
3) <u>Without</u> using your notes, draw out the different sub-topic prompts at the end of each branch. When they're all done, <u>check</u> them and make any corrections.

Bruce Willis
(obviously)

4) Use <u>pictures</u> — funny or rude ones will help you remember.
   E.g. The little aeroplane I've drawn on the "o" (out) branch for *lungs and breathing*, to me means Air Force — which helps me remember "air forced out".
5) Go over it with pen and explain all the details of each sub-topic <u>out loud</u>.

Make connections to blow the dust off your brain

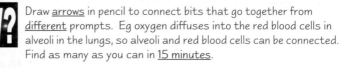

HOW? Draw <u>arrows</u> in pencil to connect bits that go together from <u>different</u> prompts. Eg oxygen diffuses into the red blood cells in alveoli in the lungs, so alveoli and red blood cells can be connected. Find as many as you can in <u>15 minutes</u>.

WHY? It gets your <u>brain working</u>, thinking about the <u>whole topic</u> instead of each sub-topic separately. It looks messy but it'll get that sack of fat in your head to wake up a bit.

Use the explosion to test yourself

1) Look at each sub-topic in <u>any order</u> and use the prompts to write out all the detail.
2) When you've done them all, <u>check</u> them, <u>correct</u> them and add any missing bits.
3) Give yourself a <u>score</u> out of five for each sub-topic... and be harsh.

0	= you didn't remember anything except maybe your own name.

5	= you didn't need to make any corrections or add anything.

4) Your scores will tell you which bits you're hot on, and which bits need work.
   You <u>really</u> know a topic when you get <u>5</u>'s for <u>all</u> the sub-topics.

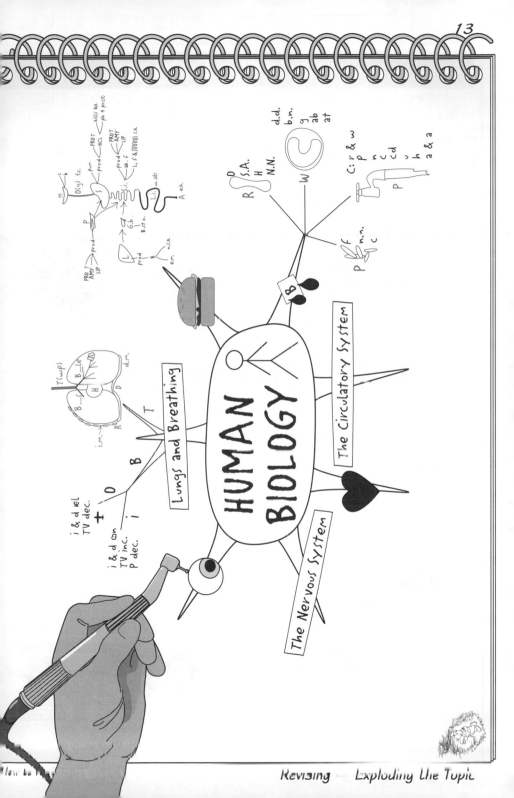

Explode the Subject

This is the same as exploding the topic, but it covers the <u>whole subject</u> — if you're doing <u>9</u> GCSEs, you'll end up with 9 of these. Just <u>9 bits of paper</u>, COVERING THE WHOLE LOT.

Draw a subject explosion

Before:

Work in <u>pencil</u> to start with.

1) Stick the name of the <u>subject</u> inside a blob in the middle of the page.

2) Draw one big branch for each <u>topic</u>.

3) Put on all the <u>sub-topic</u> branches. <u>Don't</u> draw on the prompts.

After:

4) Use <u>pictures</u>.

5) Go over it with pen. As you do so, say all the details for each sub-topic <u>out loud</u>. <u>Picture</u> the prompt in your head to help you.

6) <u>Don't</u> spend time making this look pretty.
Give yourself 30 minutes to do the whole diagram.

Use the subject explosion to test every topic

You now have one big diagram you can use to test yourself on the whole subject. You can use it to do a <u>full test</u> or a <u>quick test</u>. When you test a topic or sub-topic, put a tick next to it on your subject explosion to make sure you don't leave stuff out.

Full test

1) Pick <u>one</u> sub-topic from a topic branch. Draw the <u>prompt</u> for it on a <u>separate</u> bit of paper and then write out <u>all</u> the details underneath. Check and make any corrections.

2) Pick a sub-topic from a <u>different</u> topic branch and repeat what you did in part 1). Put a pencil tick next to each sub-topic when you've done it.

3) Keep repeating part 2) until you've done <u>all</u> the sub-topics for the <u>whole</u> subject.

Quick test

When you know a topic well, doing a quick test <u>every 2 days</u> will stop it leaking out of your brain. It's simple, just three steps:

1) Look at a sub-topic.

2) <u>Picture</u> the prompt in your head.

3) Talk through all the detail <u>out loud</u>.

If you've got a willing accomplice (or a pet) explain the topic to them. If you give them your full notes they can shout if you miss something (this last bit's trickier with a pet).

Is one of these boys the giraffe chopper?

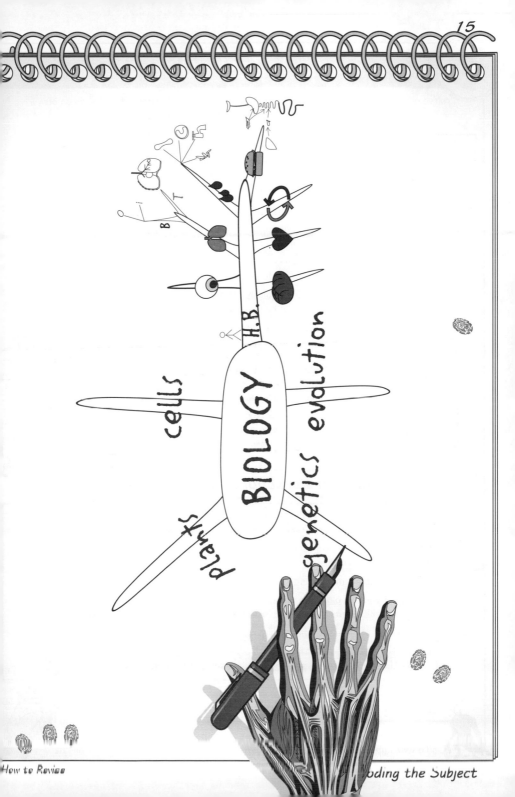

Test

You've probably noticed that you've been testing yourself throughout the revision bit — sneaky, eh! This is different though, this is <u>full-on</u> brain pummelling.

Let it all hang out — test the whole subject at once

This way of testing will reinforce your memory for <u>all</u> the topics by getting you to think about the <u>whole subject</u> at once. It's good stuff so stay awake and don't quit.

1) Pick any sub-topic from your <u>subject explosion</u> and start writing out all the details.

2) Each time you write something down, think how it could be <u>connected</u> to any other part of the subject. Look at the subject explosion to help you.

3) When you spot a <u>connection</u>, write it down and then start writing out the details of this <u>new</u> sub-topic until you spot another connection.

4) <u>Keep going</u> as long as you can, as <u>quickly</u> as you can, joining as many sub-topics as you can. This has the added bonus of being speed-writing practice for the <u>exams</u>.

5) Start a new line for each sub-topic and make a note of where it's from in the margin.

digestion	The large intestine is where excess water is absorbed from the blood. As well as water the blood also contains white blood cells.
blood	Platelets are small fragments of cells with no nucleus. They help the blood to clot at wounds, stopping you bleeding to death and micro-organisms getting in.
disease	There are three types of micro-organisms: bacteria, fungi and viruses. Bacteria are one hundreth the size of body cells.
genes	Body cells have 46 chromosomes so they are diploid.

Test yourself with workbooks and exam papers

Use workbooks (and the revision summaries in revision guides) to test each topic in <u>detail</u>. Use exam papers to practise answering <u>exam-style questions</u>.

1) <u>CGP</u> have got a whopping range of workbooks and practice papers designed for this sort of testing. Another advert, I know, but they really are the <u>dog's bollards</u>.

2) You can get old exam papers (past papers) from <u>school</u> or direct from the <u>exam boards</u>.

3) Take care if you use <u>old</u> exam papers — they may have questions covering stuff that's no longer in the exam. Don't let it freak you out. Use your course outline to check.

4) <u>Don't</u> go easy on yourself when you're marking your answers — the <u>examiners</u> won't.

5) Keep testing yourself to find out which areas you're <u>weakest</u> on. Go over those notes again and <u>re-test</u> yourself until you get it all right.

Tackling exams and demon fighting...

Go to our <u>website</u> to get advice on both of these hazardous sports.
Go to www.cgpbooks.co.uk/examtips, then find this book's home page - it's all there.

-Fin